Antanas Jonynas

The Hill

The story of a teenage Lithuanian boy during the Second World War

OR

The final thoughts of a Jewish physician before his Lithuanian patients and neighbors murdered him and his family during the Holocaust

Translated from Lithuanian by Yuval Lirov
Edited by Roy Lirov

Affinity Billing, Inc.
Marlboro, New Jersey

ISBN 978-0-9796101-0-3

Library of Congress Control Number: 2007927129

Library of Congress Subject Heading: Holocaust – Lithuania, etc.

1.1

About This Book

This story describes true events concerning little Joe Martinkus, a teenage Lithuanian farm boy, and Dr. Schmidt, a Jewish physician. Lithuanian writer Antanas Jonynas first heard the story from little Joe Martinkus himself and published this account in 1966.

My mother, Dr. Schmidt's niece, heard about these events in nearly identical detail while in the Kaunas ghetto in 1943.

When the Soviets occupied Lithuania in June 1940, they seized the property of local proprietors, arrested national leaders, and forced farmers into slavery under the guise of a land redistribution program. Deportation was used as a mechanism for enforcement of the oppressive policies, and within one year about 35,000 locals (1.3 percent of the total population) were relocated to Siberia and and Soviet Central Asia.

When the country changed hands in June 1941, the Germans abolished some of the Soviet policies and won the support of some locals. During the three-year German occupation, 94 percent of the Lithuanian Jews (220,000 individuals) were murdered, the highest percentage for any Nazi-occupied country in Europe.

The Red Army returned in 1944, and the Soviets reinstituted their oppressive policies, deporting 220,000 locals by the early 1950s.

Lithuania declared its independence in 1990, and in 2003 it became a member of the European Union. About 3,000,000 people live in Lithuania today, including about 5,000 Jews.

Antanas Jonynas published this story as the first part of his novel *In the Well* in 1966. That Jonynas penned such a piece in the hostile Soviet environment of the day was evidence of his tremendous courage, and that it escaped censorship was truly a miracle.

Yuval Lirov
December 2005

I

August 8, 1941

"The dogs must go to the dogs," cheerfully murmured Nikodemas Nakutis while sifting his fingers through a bowl of steaming potato dumplings, looking for a better morsel. At last he grabbed a dumpling from the bowl and, turning away from the table, called loudly to the shepherd boy, who had been loitering near the door. "Well, Joseph, stop sniffing around! Here, grab a whole dumpling, praise the Lord, and pray for the mistress's health."

Excited by the delicious smell, little Joe Martinkus, a lanky thirteen-year-old, sniffed aloud, swallowed quickly, and greedily wolfed down the food. Nikodemas Nakutis burst out laughing. He laughed loudly, in a grave and rich master's voice. His friend, Jurgis Meldutis, was sitting at the table and laughed along, just as loudly, but in a shrill and thin voice.

"What is the world coming to?" uttered Mr. Nakutis while turning back to the table. "Isn't it so, Mr. Meldutis? We feed dumplings to shepherds while those dogs bark that we oppress the working people . . . Shame . . . Pour another one! What are you waiting for?"

Mr. Meldutis clumsily grabbed the bottle and poured a dark, fragrant drink into elegant, thin-stemmed glasses, which no one had ever seen in Mr. Nakutis's kitchen before. In fact, Mr. Nakutis never used to eat in the kitchen and had never invited Jurgis Meldutis to his home.

All this had begun in the summer, on the day the Germans arrived and Nikodemas Nakutis and Jurgis Meldutis began wearing white bands on their sleeves and carrying rifles on their shoulders. Now they are friends and have lots to share and talk about. They meet almost every day, and almost every day they drink a few glasses of this dark, fragrant liquid, which nobody ever smelled in Mr. Nakutis's home before, although other drinks used to be served in his spacious living room not so infrequently.

"Ugh, this Yiddish mead! Horrible stuff," shuddered Mr. Nakutis, placing his thin-stemmed glass on the table and turning to his buddy. "We need solid food to match its strength." He raised himself from the bench, again pushing his fingers deep into the dumpling bowl, and glanced over his shoulder at the shepherd boy. "Have you swallowed it, Joseph? Want another one?" His large hand, holding the dumpling, stretched back, preparing to throw it. The boy ran to the table, ready to grab the delicacy.

Mrs. Nakutis appeared suddenly in the kitchen doorway. "What's wrong with you? Are you crazy?" she screamed, jumping to the table. "Feeding dumplings to shepherds! And you two gobbling down like two pigs, uninvited! What will I offer the foremen?" She shoved the teenager away with her broad back, grabbed the dumpling from her husband's outstretched hand, and tossed it back into the bowl.

"Jennie! Jennie!" she called angrily. "Where are you? Come over quickly, feed the boy, and tell the foremen . . . breakfast is getting cold."

Noisily, Mrs. Nakutis pulled open the large table drawers, took out a few spoons, knives and forks, and threw them down on the table.

"You spread yourselves out all over here with your smelly drink, taking up the whole table, and you gorge yourselves from early on. There is no room for the people," she scolded, for some reason glancing more frequently at Mr. Meldutis than at her husband.

"So where should we go?" asked Mr. Nakutis, tucking his shaved head into his shoulders. "You won't let us in the living room, and here too we are in your way. Maybe I shouldn't come home anymore?"

His voice was not yet angry or threatening, and Mrs. Nakutis, not looking for a fight, calmed herself and said, “But where shall I seat the foremen? I say, where shall I seat them?”

The steps of approaching carpenters could already be heard in the hallway. Nikodemas Nakutis’s new spacious home had been unfinished at one end for nearly two years. At last, men had started laying floors, placing windowpanes, and fixing the doors. Soon it could become livable. Then Mr. Nakutis would be able to receive his son-in-law, the newly appointed police chief of Kraziai, and other honorable and beneficial guests. Then Mrs. Nakutis would finally live in a real manor. If only the builders would not waste time, if only they finished already. She must ingratiate herself with them; they must be fed and happy.

Little Joe Martinkus has been herding at the Nakutis’s place for the third summer already. He knew how fervently Mrs. Nakutis had been dreaming about her beautiful manor. In her native village of Kareiviskes, Mrs. Nakutis was a real mistress. This was her ancestral home, her rich dowry given to her by her father, Kazimieras Dobzinskis, a wealthy landlord.

Nikodemas Nakutis was only a newcomer here. He never really cared for farming. Until just two years ago, he had received a pension in dollars from overseas, from distant America, and used to enjoy partying in Kraziai and fraternizing with the local officials and wealthier farmers.

He was well respected all around as everybody knew that he was an American soldier who had earned his pension fighting the Germans in France. He was over fifty years old, short, stocky, broad-shouldered, his head shaven. He had teasingly slanted eyes, and he loved festive gatherings. Sometimes he played his fiddle, sang loud American songs, and tirelessly recounted frightening or funny stories from his life on the other side of the ocean or from battles on the Western front. When he told of those fierce battles, it seemed as if he had been the most valiant American soldier and that not a single battle had been fought without him. And there had been no greater Casanova throughout the entire front. The French girls didn't throw themselves at anyone else more than him, although no French woman could resist any American soldier. The German girls, who could barely walk because of starvation, would sell themselves to anybody for just a loaf of bread. Needless to say, the Lithuanian girls stuck to him like bees to honey. Only, why in the world would he ever need any of those girls . . .

He could manage totally without them, if only Kazimieras Dobzinskis had not offered him two hundred acres of land along with his Leokadija. These two hundred acres of land included the Kalvariskes hill, on which he would construct the Nakutis manor, and half the world would see it. This hill, these acres, the blue-blooded origin of his wife, and even her solid, old, virginlike serious attitude, suited the American soldier. He would never take a wife for show—he needed a real mistress of the house.

But last year, Nikodemas Nakutis stopped talking about the manor and would even get angry if anybody addressed him as "Mister." The new riffraff government had carved away pieces of his farm and spoiled his business. But that was only a nightmare—a horrible and short-lived nightmare—that ended at last as all nightmares do, however frightening they might be. The German canons began roaring in the West; their steel birds, marked with fat black crosses, began circling in the sky; and every trace of the ragged government disappeared as if it had never existed in the first place.

Mr. Nakutis recalled right away that he was an American soldier, well trained in shooting both in the chest and in the back. Of course, right now there was no need to mention his American training; perhaps it was better to not even mention those battles on the Western front. Whatever had happened in the past, the German army friendship now suited him as none other in the entire world. A true soldier was always a soldier, and he always knew whom to shoot.

Nikodemas Nakutis took on a new chant —"The dogs must go to the dogs"—repeating it at every turn, slyly shutting his eyes, but no longer teasing. Instead, his eyes were filled with bitter mockery.

Everybody knew that the "dogs" were the communists, Jews, Russians, and all small landowners who had recently sprung up around Kareiviskes like mushrooms after the rain. Initially, Mr. Nakutis had defined a small landowner as one who had less than twelve acres of land. But later he understood that if only those dogs were buried, neither he nor the entire New Europe would ever have any peace. Thus, he expanded his definition to include all those who owned fifteen and even twenty acres.

"We must bury them all," he used to say to Jurgis Meldutis, "all the way up to you, right?" Mr. Meldutis owned only twenty-seven acres, and so he agreeably smiled when Mr. Nakutis reasoned about how the New Europe would not err at all by giving Mr. Meldutis another twelve or so acres. After all, Mr. Meldutis would earn this.

It wasn't hard for Jurgis Meldutis to smile, as he believed in the New Europe and in Nikodemas Nakutis. He believed because Mr. Nakutis was a powerful man with a rifle and knew how to shoot both in the chest and in the back—and his son-in-law, Antanas Motuzas, was chief of police in Kraziai and made everybody shiver in fear. Everybody shivered in front of Nikodemas Nakutis too. They even shook in front of Jurgis Meldutis, so why shouldn't Mr. Meldutis smile?

Little Joe Martinkus sat on the windowsill, slurping the borscht served by Jennie, the Nakutis's maid, and stole glances at the table. No, he wasn't looking at the dumplings, which he knew were not for him anyway. He was looking at his master, Mr. Nakutis, and at his buddy, Mr. Meldutis. Lately, these men had become chillingly mystifying and exciting to him. One could hear all sorts of talk about them in the village—the kind of talk that brings up the creeps and covers the skin with goose bumps. You could be frightened to death after chancing upon these men at night. And when they walked down the village road in unsteady step, blubbering in drunken voices, you could feel ants running down your back.

Joe had started to fear Mr. Nakutis only recently, but he had been afraid of Mr. Meldutis for as long as he could remember. All the children feared him. He just gazed at you with his large, gypsy black eyes piercing right through you and making you feel uneasy. He was tall; his large, bushy head leaned forward, with prominent jawbones protruding from a thin, swarthy face. His large, motionless eyes stared intently while his long and bony fingers were never still but always vibrated as if preparing to grab and clench something. Children had always been scared to walk past his farm, which was spread out among the bushes on the fringe of the forest. Anybody who had carelessly stepped across his damp, mounded meadows got chased by “the hunter” with a club, rake, or fork in hand.

Everybody called Mr. Meldutis a hunter, even though he rarely slinked around the edge of the forest with his single-barrel rifle in hand. Sometimes, he would hunt in the winter in fresh snow, but usually he trapped rabbits and foxes using sling nooses. Joe heard that after having caught many rabbits and foxes in the winter, Mr. Meldutis made good money for their fur pelts.

Once, Joe saw Mr. Meldutis carry a rabbit, which he had just pulled out of the trap. The little animal was still struggling, its legs kicking, while Mr. Meldutis held it in front of him by the ears, furiously tightening his thin lips as if holding his breath for the moment when he would skin the little animal. “I will skin you alive!" the hunter used to yell when chasing stray children with his club.

The four foremen—quiet, elderly men—were seated around the table and spearing the delicious dumplings with forks, cutting them with knives, and eating quietly. They were so intensely concentrated on their food and so engrossed in eating that they couldn't talk and couldn't even hear Nikodemas Nakutis. The master, however, wished to be heard and understood so the foremen would hurry and complete their construction work as soon as possible.

"We will not haggle with you like the Yids," Mr. Nakutis said obligingly, pushing the bottle toward the men. "Extra bonuses will be paid, as long as the work is not dragged on and on like a piece of burned rope."

Jurgis Meldutis laughed again, not joyfully, but in a high-pitched, broken voice. Little Joe Martinkus flinched at the sound of this laughter and at the words of Mr. Nakutis. These days, Joe had been feeling uneasy when hearing the word "Yid" or "Jew." He grew up used to grownups threatening kids with "the Jew will come . . . I will give you to a Jew, and the Jew will carry you away." But he'd always known that not a single Jew among those who had come to their village to purchase calves or collect woolen rags would ever take him away. Joe had ceased fearing these people of strange faith, who wouldn't eat pork, who were clad in roomy, shorn cloaks, and who wouldn't remove their hats, even inside the house and in front of the holy icons.

But now he feared the word "Jew." A terrible, threatening secret surrounded this word. Frightful stories were told about Jews—the Jews were herded together and shot, their belongings plundered, or Jewish toddlers grabbed by their little feet and thrown into graves or their heads smashed against concrete walls.

The Jews must have committed something terrible, and they must have angered the almighty God. But even so, everybody in the village said that they did not deserve such cruelty. Joe thought the same. Somewhere, not far away from Kelme, in the Kupres forest, huge graves were dug and Jews were shot there. They were brought from Kraziai, herded along the Karalienes highway, stripped naked, and lined up alongside the graves. They clustered in small groups with their families, the children and the mothers hugging their men, and they screamed—they screamed on and on. The village women heard their last screams: "*Oy tattale, oy mammale . . .*"

They said that Nikodemas Nakutis had been there in the Kupres forest—together with Jurgis Meldutis—and they were shooting, so they said, even though Mrs. Nakutis would jump up to argue and deny every time she heard village women talking about her husband. But little Joe Martinkus had seen Jewish belongings show up in the Nakutis home . . . and those thin-stemmed glasses from which Mr. Nakutis and Mr. Meldutis drank, they also used to be Jewish.

Then they said that at night, the Jews who remained alive or the wounded ones who somehow recovered, they climbed out of their graves and crawled through the woods, leaving bloody tracks . . . even those who were killed and dead, they sometimes rose from the graves and roamed the woods and the Karalienes highway at night and scared people. How could you tell them apart, the living and the ghosts?

"Have you forgotten your borscht? Or maybe you have already fallen asleep, you meat-head!"

Joe felt a sudden poke in his back from Mrs. Nakutis and nearly dropped the spoon from his hand.

"No way will he get done eating . . . the people have come and gone, but he is still here," she continued.

The foremen were already leaving the table, thanking the hostess and wiping their mouths. To avoid listening to Mr. Nakutis's nagging any further, they didn't even stay around to smoke a cigarette. Who cared to haggle with a Jew killer?

Jurgis Meldutis stood up, infuriated. His dark face turned even darker while red sparks began flickering in his black eyes. "Doctor or no doctor, he is a Yid." Mr. Meldutis lifted his heated glance at Nikodemas Nakutis. "The pastor is shrewd like the devil himself. Some advocate. Imagine! He will keep the gold for himself. You will all see."

Little Joe Martinkus understood that the hunter was talking about Dr. Schmidt, the only surviving Jew in Kraziai. The pastor himself had interceded for Dr. Schmidt, and the townswomen too, with tears in their eyes, had begged for his life.

"Keep your hands off the doctor!" yelled Mrs. Nakutis. "He took care of little Rimute all winter and brought her back to life from meningitis." The mistress had been about to leave, but now she returned, sat by the table, and intently watched her husband.

Suddenly, Mr. Nakutis got mad. "Joseph, you bastard!" he yelled in a hoarse-creaking voice. "Why are you still messing around and getting on the mistress's nerves? You've swallowed your meal, now hurry back to the animals!"

Mrs. Nakutis too turned to the shepherd, grabbed the bowl from the windowsill, and wrenched the spoon away from Joe's hand.

“Hurry up and go already,” she scolded him impatiently, but not as angrily as Mr. Nakutis. “Valius is just loafing around up there on the hill, and it is time to bring the rye in. Tell him to get here right away.”

II

Little Joe Martinkus could run. For the seventh summer, he was herding other people's animals. He'd been continuously running since he started herding when he was six. But he was also beginning to learn. For instance, it wasn't such a big deal if the master yelled. They all yelled—the nice ones and the nasty ones, those who talked sweetly when they wanted something from him and also the silent ones who counted their words better than money. The boy had gotten used to them yelling.

Now everything was boring. The masters were boring, the animals were boring, and the shepherd job was just unbearable. He was no longer a little boy; he understood everything, but everybody still shoved him around like a silly child. If Mrs. Nakutis just tried to pull the bowl of borscht away from him . . . and even if she was very angry, he wouldn't let her get away with it. He would make her afraid and ashamed. Joe got off the porch, kicked some wood shavings left behind by the carpenters, wiped his mouth with his sleeve, snorted angrily, and set out to the gate.

His brother Valius was waiting for him on the hill. Mrs. Nakutis would like to think that Valius had been waiting impatiently. Her rye became as dry as gunpowder, begging for the barn to avoid getting caught in a downpour.

But Joe's brother Valius couldn't care less about her rye. Right now he was lying on his back and looking up at the very small white clouds up in the August sky, hoping little Joe would not hurry and would let him lie there a little longer. There would be plenty of time to get exhausted during the long summer day for a young farmhand who had turned sixteen only in the spring. And then, Valius wasn't that healthy to begin with, having had an incurable sore on his leg since childhood, a sore that kept reopening from time to time. He had to lie down and rest more than others.

After reaching the gate, the little shepherd thought of something, stomped his feet, turned around, and ran into the backyard. Joe's sleeping place was on the second floor of the barn, in a narrow garret filled with hay. There he hid his treasure, under the hard pillow stuffed with tow. Last night, he'd stuck it there and forgotten about it. He'd never forgotten it, but today he had. Yet near the gate, he'd felt that something was missing. His pocket felt strangely empty, as there was nothing thumping against his thigh.

For three weeks now, little Joe Martinkus had not parted from his little treasure. He'd slept with it and run around with it. It was such a beautiful little thing—round, even, shiny in the sunlight. If he touched it with his hand, he got a pleasant, cool sensation as its soft evenness tickled his skin. If he ran with it in his pocket, it thumped against his thigh . . . *thump, thump, thump* . . . as if somebody were beating out a running rhythm for him on a little drum.

It was such an unusual trophy. None of his friends had anything like it, and none ever would. Many would like to have such a thing. Uncle Bernotas—little Joe could not keep from laughing when he thought of Uncle Bernotas. A grown man, a blacksmith, he made such a fool of himself!

A fierce tank battle had taken place near the village of Klibaliai in June. Many vehicles —some damaged, others simply stuck in the swamp—had remained there since. Enterprising locals had picked up all sorts of things from those vehicles: clocks, batteries, magnets, buckets with gasoline. But Uncle Bernotas had only wished to shoot the tank's cannon. He'd wanted nothing else, and he couldn't resist this urge to shoot the cannon. He'd tried every possible way, but nothing worked. Then he'd brought a long awl and a hammer, fitted the awl on the capsule, and hit it with the hammer. The sudden shot had shocked the entire countryside. The tank had moved, rolling down the slope and falling into the swamp. Bystanders had pulled the unconscious Uncle Bernotas out. He'd lost two fingers on his left hand and his face was covered with little, ugly black dots. "Gunner" was his new nickname in Klibaliai.

Little Joe Martinkus had been able to get on top of the tank turret and down the hatch to reach the cannon. He couldn't get out the shell, but he'd been able to remove the capsule —the magnificent, shiny capsule—which he'd been carrying around without showing to anybody. Sometimes he tossed it around, tucked it under the pillow at night, and then returned it to his pocket in the morning. Of course, had he shown it to anybody, everybody would get scared and they would take it away from him. Oh! Mrs. Nakutis would die from fright. But Joe wasn't afraid. Someday he would have some more free time, when the cows had finished feeding and had lain down to chew their cud, and he would take apart the capsule and discover what was inside. Then the capsule wouldn't be a secret any longer and he would tell everybody about it— including Uncle Bernotas, that skillful blacksmith who, though he'd lost two fingers, still couldn't uncover the secret of the capsule.

As the little shepherd stepped out of the barn, he couldn't resist pulling the little object out of his pocket and rolling it around in the sunlight. It shone so wonderfully in the sunlight.

“Joe, what have you got there?” asked little Rimute, appearing out of nowhere, in a curious, almost accusing voice.

Nimbly, the shepherd tucked his treasure back into his pocket.

“Nothing! You’re imagining things!” he yelled at the skinny, pale little girl with thin braids, wearing a blue, freshly washed frock.

“I saw it! You got something . . . something shiny,” insisted the girl, determined not to let anyone deceive her. Little Rimute was eleven years old, nosy, and spoiled. All last winter, she’d been very ill, and everybody around the house had indulged her—everybody, even Joseph, who at times had felt very sorry for her and feared she would die.

But now he was angry with Rimute. He was angry because Rimute never did any work. And because she was so nosy and so spoiled. If she liked something, she needed to have it right away.

“I have nothing. Go away!” he said angrily, trying to get on his way.

“You’ve got something!” shouted Rimute angrily. “You must have stolen something from my dad, and I will tell him on you.”

“I’ve got nothing!” yelled the shepherd and, avoiding the girl, he started running across the yard.

“Mom!” screamed Rimute. “The shepherd stole—”

Mrs. Nakutis appeared on the porch and clapped her hands. “Oh, Lord, he’s still here,” she complained. “What’s wrong my little girl?”

As Rimute talked to her mother, Joe was already far away, running as fast as he could to his cows and his brother Valius. “My little girl, my little girl,” Joe mocked Mrs. Nakutis in his mind.

In truth, Mrs. Leokadija Nakutis had never had any kids of her own. Little Rimute was the daughter of her deceased sister. Whenever little Joe got angry with his mistress, he thought about her troubles with kids. Rimute was Mrs. Nakutis’s third adopted daughter. Emilija, her first adoptee, had married Motuzas, the police chief, quite some time ago.

Last year, when the working class had still ruled the country, Motuzas had to hide far away. Now he’d returned to become the police chief of Kraziai. But he missed Emilija because last spring the Soviets had deported her, together with her children, to distant Siberia. Whenever Mrs. Nakutis wept for Emilija, her Mr. Nakutis would get angry and say that all dogs must be shot for this crime.

Brone, the second adopted daughter, had pulled a trick on Leokadija just before the arrival of the Soviets. While the Nakutis family had had high hopes for her continued education in the city, she wouldn’t and couldn't return to school in the fall because during her summer vacation, she had befriended Augustinas, their farmhand, who'd gotten her pregnant. Both senior Nakutises were shamed and enraged because of the dishonor, but they could change nothing; Brone had told them she couldn't live without Augustinas, and they had married soon after. At first they had wandered away, but later Mrs. Nakutis let them move into a hut that had been built for summer hired hands. "There is plenty of work all year long, and we need help," Mrs. Nakutis had explained to her husband, who was still mad at his shameless and ungrateful daughter.

Yet last summer, when the Soviets had begun carving away the lands of the wealthy landlords, Mr. Nakutis seemed to have a change of heart. He had gone to Augustinas and made him a generous offer: "Dear son-in-law, we are now family. Take half of my land, and we both will become *kulaks*[1]. We will each have one hundred acres. After the punks take

---

1 *kulak, "fist"*, literally meaning tight-fisted; a pejorative term used in Soviet political language, referring to peasants who owned larger farms and used hired labor. During Stalinist Soviet rule, the kulaks were subject to one of three fates: death sentence, labor camps, or deportation to labor settlements. Hundreds of thousands of alleged kulaks and their families were executed or deported to Siberia and Soviet Central Asia, while their property was expropriated. *yl*

away twenty-five acres from each of us, we will still own one hundred and fifty together."

Augustinas Cetkunas may have been lazy and slow, but he wasn't stupid. "No, you alone can keep this honor. Besides, the new government will give me land anyway. I do not need to become a *kulak*. If you can't stomach so much land, why don't you give it away on your own? I will take twenty-five acres, but no more."

Mr. Nakutis was angry; he called Augustinas a treacherous snake, but at the end he gave him the land and even helped him put up some new farm buildings. And as soon as the Germans arrived, he madly chased away all the punks who had been settled on his land by the Soviets. Yet he did not touch his son-in-law. He angrily eyed him up and down, but did not touch him, neither by hand nor by word. Mrs. Nakutis didn't allow it. Perhaps Mrs. Nakutis was rough with everybody, but she cared deeply for her adopted daughters. Her feelings would be badly hurt whenever somebody said, "What sort of daughters are they? You can pick them along the highway for a dime a dozen." She would poke out anyone's eyes for such words, and everybody in the village and in the entire county knew that all too well. And so her daughters were also the best way to her heart.

Little Rimute, the third adopted daughter, had spent the entire last summer sick in bed. By fall, nobody had expected her to get well anymore. Mrs. Nakutis used to spend all her nights next to her, crying her eyes out, and little Joe had felt sorry for both little Rimute and even Mrs. Nakutis. He would love to have replaced his mistress for a night so she could get some sleep. It would have been easy for him to give little Rimute a drink of water or tell her fairy tales. But Mrs. Nakutis wouldn't let anybody near her daughter, even though Rimute wasn't her real daughter.

Several times a month, Dr. Schmidt used to come from Kraziai, examine the patient, and spend many hours calming Mrs. Nakutis and writing prescriptions. Everybody knew that Dr. Schmidt had saved Rimute. Mrs. Nakutis felt forever grateful to the tall and not at all old doctor. Mr. Nakutis felt grateful too, and he had even invited the doctor to join him for dinner. But Dr. Schmidt had not joined him at the table, perhaps because, as a Jew, he wasn't supposed to eat Catholic food. Imagine if Mr. Nakutis had deceived him and fed him bacon. Mr. Nakutis loved deceiving people for kicks and giggles and making fun of them later. Dr. Schmidt was too smart and prudent for Mr. Nakutis's pranks.

Little Rimute was fine and healthy now. She had turned into a spoiled child, and now everybody had to meet her every wish. No way would Joe show her his capsule. Rimute would tell everybody right away, they would all get very upset and Mr. Nakutis would thrash him. Mr. Nakutis was so angry these days . . .

Thump, thump, thump went the small, hard, and heavy metal object against his thigh. Little Joe Martinkus was running up the hill, feeling the loud and pleasant thumping of the capsule. Of course the capsule could be dangerous, but Joe wasn't as dumb as Uncle Bernotas. Joe was careful—very careful. One day, when he had more time, after the cows had been fed and had lain down to chew their cud, he would cautiously take apart the capsule and tell everybody its secret.

Oh, when little Joe grew up, he would figure out many secrets. He would become an inventor. He would construct trucks, tanks, and even large machines. He would start with a bicycle. Bicycles were easy. He just needed some iron . . . getting rubber for the tires might be the hardest. Joe once saw a bicycle up close and even touched it with his own hands. He could determine its construction with his eyes shut.

Mr. Nakutis's hill was steep and long. Your legs gave out and you ran short of breath while climbing it. Joe always needed a rest when climbing Mr. Nakutis's hill. He needed to see where Rimute was right at this moment.

Mr. Nakutis's land had several hills. Even his new farmhouse was built on a hill, except that hill was bare and not as steep. A few willows were planted around the barn, but they still were as thin as horsewhips and, from a distance, the entire Nakutis yard was easily visible. He could see Rimute standing near the porch. She seemed as tiny as a blue pea. No, she had not chased Joe. She knew she couldn't catch up with him anyway.

Now Joe saw Mr. Nakutis and Mr. Meldutis leaving through the porch. Their rifle barrels looked like knitting needles from a distance. They stopped in front of Rimute. Perhaps she was telling them about the shining thing stolen by the shepherd boy. Mr. Nakutis would believe her. He thought the entire county was full of thieves.

Joe felt cold and uneasy. He resumed climbing the hill quickly, avoiding rocks and bushes. *Thump, thump, thump*—the metal object thumped against his thigh, although not as loudly and not as frequently as before. Should Joe hide it here under the bush? He could pick it up later. But Mr. Nakutis wouldn't believe that Joe had nothing at all and would get even angrier and begin beating up Joe for real. Or he might threaten to shoot

Joe. Whenever Mr. Nakutis was drunk, he would threaten to shoot him.

The shepherd looked furtively behind. No, Mr. Nakutis did not believe Rimute. Or maybe he had decided to find the shepherd later tonight.

Still worried, Joe's eyes followed Mr. Nakutis and Mr. Meldutis's path across the swampy and mounded meadow. First they crossed a small and ugly brook, and next they reached the Pasiles road, where they disappeared with their rifles slung across their shoulders. They took the same path every day, and nobody knew when and in what shape they would return . . . A drunk Mr. Nakutis wouldn't listen if Joe were empty-handed. Joe would have to show his capsule.

"Valius!" yelled out the shepherd angrily, as if he had been searching for his brother for a long hour. A shepherd too could get angry. He too needed to let out his frustration. Pretending he hadn't heard his brother's reply, he yelled again, "Valius, where are you?"

"Are you blind, Joe?" laughed his brother, lifting up from the grass behind the tree. "Can't you spot a man on a hill?"

"Can't spot, can't spot," mocked the little shepherd. "Mrs. Nakutis is going mad in the yard waiting for you. Move your lazy bones already."

Valius was still drowsy. He stretched waving his arms. “Relax, she’ll be fine,” he said calmingly to Joe. “We’ll have plenty of time to get tired. The day is still young and there is tons of rye.”

Valius picked up his old, frayed cap from the ground and began walking downhill with the slow gait of an old man, somewhat dragging his leg that was tortured by the sore from his chronic infection.

Valius’s slow movement always irritated Joe. He blushed with shame whenever others called Valius an “old man.” It felt as if they were making fun of Joe too. How can a sixteen-year-old be so stiff and chatty? Valius could lecture forever, like an old man with no outlet for all his accumulated wisdom. Joe was tempted to throw a stone at his brother’s back to make him jump and hurry up, but then he noticed Valius’s ailing leg and felt sorry, his anger subsiding.

III

No, little Joe Martinkus would become neither a blacksmith nor an inventor. He liked the machines only from time to time. Music was his true love. Joe even liked Mr. Nakutis when the man played his fiddle during the long winter nights. Last winter he had played often, feeling sad and worried. The Soviets had taken much of his land. Nobody had visited him anymore. Little Rimute had been sick, and so Mr. Nakutis used to try to cheer her up with his fiddle.

But the fiddle was not the most beautiful music. And the harmonica that Uncle Bernotas used to play did not make really beautiful music either. Once, Joe had heard an accordion being played at the Nakutises' house. It had been quite a long time ago—maybe even two years ago—but Joe could still remember the unusually moving, longing music, which sometimes wept in sorrow and sometimes laughed in joy. It played like an organ in multiple voices, but it sounded happier and faster. Joe had heard the organ music only once, in the Pasiles church. He'd never had time for church; he was always busy with his animals, even on Sundays. Who cared if the little shepherd ever prayed or not?

But in the fields, Joe could often hear people sing. Sometimes he heard women sing on their return home from the fields, but he didn't like their songs. Joe's heartbeat would come to a halt when the farmhands of Klibaliai sang. He would freeze listening to a sad, longing melody calling out for someone, perhaps complaining about something, drifting across the fields, uninterrupted, endless, ever extending far away, reaching and melting into the woods or fading away into the blue fog, reaching up high in the sky. People didn't get together to sing in Kareiviskes because their houses were too far apart. But it had been easy for the Klibaliai farmhands to get together because their houses were clustered together, each owning only small pieces of land. Sometimes Joe got so homesick for his native Klibaliai, he was ready to run those seven kilometers straight home, forgetting his animals, just to listen to the farmhands' singing. He never ran anywhere, of course, and he did not attempt to escape anymore. A long time ago, when he had still been young and foolish, he once tried to escape, but he wouldn't try again. He didn't want to see his mother crying and so upset again.

As for the songs, if he really missed them, he could hear them in his mind. He just needed to sit very quietly on the hill and listen very hard. The song would rise slowly inside him, then start filling the air, resonate above the hill, and drift across the fields. Joe didn't notice himself singing loudly, so loudly and so beautifully that even the cows stopped in their tracks to listen to him.

He would grow up to be a singer. He would be a great singer, above all comparisons. Many of the farmhands in Klibaliai sang beautifully, both in deep bass and ringing tenor voices, vibrant with tension. But Joe would sing even better and more loudly, and his songs would bring people joy and sadness, and bring tears to their eyes. Everybody would listen to his voice and would ask for nothing else—just the song, an endless song, melting in the distant woods and in the blue fog, and yet never drowning away. When he sang, it would seem that all of the Klibaliai farmhands were singing together, a million voices, the entire world.

But first he must grow up. Little Joe Martinkus was so tired of being just a shepherd. Everything became a nuisance—the cows, the fields, the rain, the autumn frosts, the freezing dew, so cold as to burn his feet, the lugging of pails, the dragging of hay nets, and oversized wooden clogs. When Joe grew up, nobody would push him around anymore. Nobody would pull his food out of his hands like Mrs. Nakutis did today. Of course she wouldn't pull the food away from a grown farmhand. She wouldn't dare to slap anybody's back . . . never. Why did growing up take so long?

His mother had always told him, "Patience, my child," as if she were oblivious to how tired he was from being patient. "Patience, my child. Patience." Her tired voice still rang in his ears, despairing and infuriating him at the same time. He had grown up hearing and hating these words since he was six years old. Perhaps she hadn't known any other words? "Patience, my child. Patience," she had repeated last year, even more frequently and more hopefully.

Mrs. Martinkus had been given forty-five acres in the village of Adomaiciai. Izidorius, Joe's oldest brother, had quit his job as a farmhand last winter and hurried to get married because he was determined to become a master of his own. And starting this autumn, he wouldn't let Joe continue as a shepherd anymore.

The newly appointed landlords, without houses or animals of their own, had high hopes and patiently looked forward to better lives. But just when their dreams had been about to turn real, the Germans came, the former landlords reclaimed their lands, and the settlers had to run away, lucky to be alive. Nobody knew what to expect anymore. Joe yearned only to grow up and become a farmhand. Once he grew up, he'd think about things on his own. No more "Patience, my child."

Angry and still arguing with his mother in his mind, the shepherd rounded up the scattered cows and finally calmed down after taking out his anger on a spotted cow that was stuck in the clover field. He had always liked the hill, regardless of how upset he was. There was only one such hill in the entire world. After all, this hill belonged to Joe. Not to Mr. Nakutis. Not to Mrs. Nakutis. Just to Joe alone. Little Joe Martinkus knew the hill better than anybody else and loved it more than anybody else. He knew how far he could see from its top. He knew how steep its southern slope was, and how hot it got here during summers. Joe was familiar with every tree and every bush. It was so nice to lie under the wide-branched oak. The cows too found themselves shady spots and lay down, quiet, full, and sleepy. Midday found the sunbathed fields still in meditation. It seemed that even the leaves ceased to rustle and everything around went to rest . . .

Surprisingly, the hill had no name. Even stranger yet, the hill had no legends or tales told about it. It was strange, because during the midday rest, the hill became very mysterious. Joe stood on the hill like a giant who could be seen by everybody from afar and who owned all the fields, woods, meadows, streams, and brooks in the wet and mounded valleys. Should the giant start singing, he would be heard from a distance, and thousands of people would run to the miraculous hill. They would crane their necks to look at him, and Joe would loudly tell them, "Enough suffering! Come to my hill, and I will give you all big loaves of bread, bacon, shoes with leather soles, and a round cake on Sundays."

But the giant remained silent. He was under a spell, and he couldn't sing or speak. For now, the giant was turned into a little shepherd who had to get up early before the sunrise. In the early morning, the magic hill was still covered in a thick fog when Joe herded Mr. Nakutis's cows there. Large drops of heavy morning dew accumulated on the grass. He walked barefoot.

As the fall approached, the morning dew grew heavier and cooler. The giant-turned-shepherd boy yelled out through the fog, and his sonorous, childish voice replied from the foot of the hill in a series of receding echoes, making the hill appear to Joe even more mysterious and private. But he could barely wait for the sun to climb above the trees and for the dew to start warming up and stop hurting his feet. That's when somebody would come to call him for breakfast . . .

Little Joe Martinkus was lucky to own a hill. All the shepherds who herded animals in the thicket-covered mounded mashes envied Joe. After all, a hill was closer to the sky and to the sun.

The sun liberated itself from the fog and rose up. The caraway seeds ripening on the slope grew more fragrant by the hour, and the ground didn't feel as cold and damp when stepped upon by a bare foot. The fallow land had dried, the thyme plants about to stop blooming grew more aromatic, the grasshoppers played more noisily, and the loud song of an oriole echoed in a continuous melody. The golden-winged singer must have been somewhere nearby in the dewy, ploughed fields or in the bushes. The boy jumped up from the fallow ground to look around for the wonderful bird. Its song excited him and invited him somewhere far, unseen, and very beautiful. It wasn't easy to spot the bird. His gaze wandered by the sunlit treetops to the valley spread out further away, beyond the hill, to the distant woods that rested against the sky. His eyes opened wider as the oriole's song described the beauty in front of him. The sparkling morning dew ran down into sand, and the trees ran too, as if they came alive, waving their branches and enjoying the sun. They ran without running away, and the open valley awaited them, flooded with sunlight and decked with colorful shawls. Yellow, waxlike stubble fields, browned shocks, and small green meadows were squeezed in between the dark brown plowed fields, glistening in the sun.

The valley stretched all the way to the sky, where it was met by blue, smoky forests, silent, motionless, and mysterious. And a vast transparent sky covered the hills, the endless valley, and the woods looming in the distance. A faded blue, still sea could be seen through the dome of the sky. It had a small, nearly invisible white spot. Joe knew it must be a cloud and it must be very high up.

His little heart throbbed in excitement. What was happening to him? Why was it that everyday things around him suddenly turned into such beauty? Perhaps he himself was changing too? Maybe he was growing big and strong? Maybe he would hear no more "Patience, my child"?

While his heart was beating, his eyes filled with tears. He wanted to say, "Mummy, look how beautiful everything around is!" He felt strong now, walking down the hill in big strides, with his arms spread out like those running trees.

He recognized the horned head of the spotted cow in front of him. The cunning cow was trying to sneak back into the clover field. A flash of anger flared up in the shepherd's heart. Joe grabbed a whip and yelled, "Get back, you animal! I'll kill you!" The cow, sensing real danger and the boy's ability to kill, ran back to the herd.

The wonderful surroundings faded away. Sniffling, Joe rounded up the animals, threw himself on his stomach onto the fallow ground, and avoided looking at anything. After all, none of it was real—there were no running trees, endless valleys, or mysterious woods in the real world. The only reality was that he must remain patient. Joe wiped away his tears with the back of his hand.

He remembered a hard object pressing against his thigh. His capsule! He turned onto his back, pulled the capsule from his pocket, and tossed it up in the air. The cold metal shone in the sun. It had an austere but beautiful shine.

Joe sat up and carefully examined his toy. How would he take it apart? Could it be done at all? There must be a way to look inside . . . if he bumped it against something hard, would it break apart?

Joe found a rock and squatted down to examine the capsule again from very close. There was nothing to fear. For two weeks already, he'd walked and slept, never separating from this capsule.

"I will try this end," he said, concentrating and striking the capsule with all his might against the rock.

Nothing happened. No explosion. No sound. Just silence. The tree leaves rustled quietly, and the oriole, apparently having flown further away, whistled quietly too. Heavy dewdrops fell down from the bush onto the little shepherd's face.

Now Joe felt himself sitting, which surprised him because he remembered squatting. Very heavy dewdrops kept flowing down onto his face from the bush. They ran down his face and started dripping onto his chest, building up into a stream and dripping onto the ground. Joe lifted his right hand, wiped his face, and felt a strange stickiness. It must be blood. Blood! But he didn't see any blood.

Joe noticed he was in the dark. Complete darkness surrounded him. Was it evening already, and had he just lain down here for the entire day? Blood! Joe was terrified. He let out a fearful scream. His own scream frightened him even more, and he felt his body melting, sinking somewhere, and falling into a deep well.

IV

A two-horse wagon stood alongside a shock of rye. White linen sheets lined the bottom of the wagon to keep grains from spilling on the ground. Alex Girnius lifted the heavy sheaves of rye from the ground and carefully handed them over to Valius, who arranged them in the wagon facing inward. They both were silent and totally engrossed in their work, as if hauling grain crops was immensely pleasing them. The August sun was rising in the sky; it was big and hot, mindful of its sacred duty to assist the farmer to collect dry grain from the fields. The fields were quiet, calm, pleasantly tired and satisfied, having delivered a harvest without disappointing the farmers. Seldom did the rye yield as good a crop in the lowland hills and damp meadows as it had this year. These days, bread cost more than gold. The war was easier for peasants with bread. Bread was always needed, but during wartime, it became the only solace for men.

Alex Girnius was a strong farmhand. He was strong and taciturn. He effortlessly lifted the heavy sheaf from the ground and spun it around on his fork in the air. His receiver had no time to look around or wipe sweat. Alex didn't like to wait. He liked to work rhythmically, like in a dance. Rhythmic work kept him from tiring.

It was hard for Valius to work with Alex in silence, without rest, without mopping his sweat, but to admit being tired was even harder. Alex wouldn't say anything, but his half-angry, half-regretful look alone would show his disdain for being paired with an immature boy. Alex's face would cloud over and his eyes would become bored, displeased with himself and his work. He might even throw the fork aside, sit on the ground, leaning his shoulders against a tree, and lazily roll a cigarette. His gaze would roam across the fields, totally ignoring Valius. To win Alex's approval, Valius thought of nothing else while he worked, trying to catch his older friend's eye and to guess whether Alex was disappointed.

They continued together until lunchtime, one working easily and smoothly while the other was tired and stressed out, but both appreciated the importance of their work, sensing the deep, solemn calm of harvesting rye. They would work the same way after lunch and tomorrow, and the day after tomorrow, ignorant of their surroundings, their masters, and the final destination of the bread they brought forth. Work that turned into music ruled the man and became the essence of his goals and his entire life.

Suddenly, a powerful explosion shook the fields, frightening the quietly standing horses and forcing Valius to grab the edge of the wagon. Startled, Alex lifted his head and listened attentively.

"Who is shooting?" Valius sounded worried, but Alex had already returned to his sheaf.

"The shepherds must be blowing up something," replied Alex, passing a new sheaf to Valius.

"No, not shepherds," disagreed Valius. "That was a huge explosion." He would like to show off his smarts and to frighten Alex a bit, but suddenly he spotted the cows running down the hill, and he froze in fear. "There," he said, unable to catch his breath. "What's on with those cows?"

A muddled premonition propelled Valius from the wagon and made him race to the hill, where he had left his brother a few hours before. Alex didn't scold Valius, but followed him in his wide stride, still holding his fork in his hands. Cows did not run around without a reason. The explosion must have happened at the top of this hill.

"Joe! Joe!" called Valius again and again.

"Ah!" he heard a loud scream from the hill. The hill was close, but nobody answered Valius anymore. Valius just noticed the tranquility of the August midday and the weak, monotonous grasshopper chirp in the grass.

A light, grayish blue smoke rose from the grass at the very top of the hill. Alex smelled the sweet odor of blood and saw a little boy in a strangely curled position, his hands covering his face. He couldn't tell little Joe's hands apart from the face.

"What did you do to yourself, Joey?" moaned Valius in a frightened voice while kneeling down, shaking his brother's shoulder and looking at his disfigured body.

"Hey, you. Calm down and leave him alone!" sternly admonished Alex. "Run to Mrs. Nakutis and ask her for a wagon."

Valius turned around and looked at Alex, bewildered, with eyes full of tears.

"We must pick him up," Alex softened, embarrassed by his own angry voice. "We can't leave him here . . . his blood will drain away very quickly."

Alex heard the power in his voice, and it sounded to him as if it were booming from inside a barrel. For the first time, he thought that his voice might scare people, and he was glad he didn't talk much. "Run. Hurry up, I'm telling you," he urged Valius very quietly, and then Alex turned and ran down the hill himself. He didn't mean to run and he didn't think about it, but his legs began carrying him on their own back to the rye shocks where he'd left the horses and the wagon.

Up until now, nobody had ever seen Alex run. He had always walked with a heavy, uniform step, swaying from side to side like the pendulum of an antique wall clock. From a distance, his gait appeared as if he were just swaying in place, but anybody next to him had to run to keep up. Now Alex Girnius was running, ungracefully, heavily, as if his large, rigid legs were made of oak blocks that required yanking out of the ground and throwing them far in front of him.

He was not going to ask permission from Mrs. Nakutis; she wouldn't dare prevent him from taking the horses. Alex knew how to forget he had a mistress, although it happened very seldom, only if something really important came up. Right now, nobody would be able to remind him that he was just a hired hand who must get permission—his powerful, large arms were already tossing the sheaves out from the wagon right onto the ground. It didn't matter anymore how much of the grain might get scattered on the ground. Time was the only thing that mattered now. Standing up in the wagon, right on the white sheets, and stepping over the remaining pieces of rye with his wooden soles, Alex swung the long reins and flogged the horses. The wagon dashed, jumping across clogs and rocks; it flew, without any road, across the stubble field, sometimes catching on shocks of rye. Alex turned the horses onto a narrow path leading to the hill. He didn't know where he would take the injured shepherd, but he knew he must get there quickly and not leave him lying in the field.

Alex lifted Joe in his arms, cuddling him to his chest that was covered with a sleeveless shirt. The farmhand's rough skin felt the warmth of the child's body and the boy's sporadic heartbeat. Alex felt as if he'd picked up a small, frightened, featherless bird that had fallen out of its nest.

The shepherd boy moaned, letting his hands fall off his face. Alex looked away. He knew there was no face anymore, and he avoided looking at what was left. He avoided looking at the boy's dangling arms too. He only felt that the arms were soft, sticky, and wet. There might be not much left of his arms either.

Alex had never carried children around. He had never desired to carry any children. He nearly hated little children. But now he carried this young teenager easily, carefully, and without even thinking about it. Slowly, he laid Joe down at the bottom of the wagon, on the clean white sheet that had been prepared earlier for bringing home the rye from the fields. He placed some packed straw under the boy's head. The child lay on his back, with his head facing the sky, which still had a few small white clouds.

Slowly, the wagon started moving. Alex held the reins tightly, restraining the horses from trotting down the steep hill. Joe was silent. Alex was silent too, swaying from side to side, more slowly than usual.

The news about the shepherd hurt in an explosion had already reached the entire village. People who had been working in the nearby fields threw their forks away, left the half-loaded wagons behind, and ran to the hill. They ran to the wagon, leaned over its side, and looked at the child's face, chest, and hands. They groaned and tried talking to Alex, who was busy clutching and straining the reins. He didn't answer, seemingly oblivious to their talk about exposed flesh and an uncontrollable flow of blood. The talk made him more nauseous than the smell of blood.

Mrs. Nakutis approached the wagon in a hurry, lumbering and leaning forward with her entire large body. Her eyebrows were knitted, and her lips were tightly pursed together.

"Jesus Maria!" her voice belied anger and reproach—reproach of the shepherd who'd abandoned his herd and of the farmhand who'd diverted her horses from important work without asking for permission.

"Jesus Maria!" she repeated in a stricter tone, trying to catch Alex's eye. But terror sprang in her eyes, and she clutched her head in her hands as soon as she saw the bottom of the wagon.

"Jesus Maria . . . he's been torn apart. He is hopeless. He will die without a chance to light a candle."

Little Rimute observed the changed expression of her mother's face and guessed the cause. "Mommy, was it a capsule? I saw how it glistened . . . oh, it glistened a whole lot."

"Lord help us," exclaimed Mrs. Nakutis as she realized how close she'd been to having the explosion happen right in her backyard near her child. She exchanged a few words with neighbors, sighed a couple of times, and, as if suddenly remembering, turned to the farmhand and asked softly, almost apologetically, "So, where are you taking him?"

"To Kraziai," replied Alex, who wondered himself until right this moment about where to take the injured boy.

Mrs. Nakutis sighed and shook her head in disagreement. "He will not make it that far. He will die in the wagon," she said.

"We will take him anyway," Alex replied quietly and confidently, as if he were the only one with a solid grasp of the problem at hand.

"Just return the horses as quick as you can . . . what a day!" agreed Mrs. Nakutis, looking at the peacefully shining sun in the afternoon sky.

The farmhand nodded, letting the mistress know he should not waste any more time than necessary.

Hesitating for a moment, she crossed herself. After all, even an insignificant little shepherd had a soul. Perhaps her holy sign of the cross might help his salvation. Nobody took the likes of him to confession . . .

Now Alex and Valius followed the wagon on foot, Alex holding the reins and Valius limping clumsily along and holding onto the edge of the wagon. Alex focused on the road; any hole could turn the wagon on its side, and any stone could bump the wounded boy.

Valius's eyes stared at the sheet on the bottom of the wagon. He wasn't looking at his brother, instead focusing on the sheet. It was no longer white, except for a small, dry area of linen at the foot. The sheet was a reddish black color. At the top, near Joe's head, the rye was bloody too. A large, long, ripe ear of rye with widely spread-out beads was full of blood. The beads had darkened and the grain inside must have been swollen and full of blood, making the beads appear thick and large.

"All bread is bloody this year," thought Valius to himself. He wished to share this thought with Alex, but he knew that Alex didn't like this kind of talk. Alex might just spit in anger. Other people didn't like Valius talking like this either. Nothing useful came out of such talk . . .

"Drink! I'm thirsty," moaned Joe, helplessly flailing at the sticky sheets.

Valius bent over the edge of the wagon, recoiled, and looked around in bewilderment. There were no houses near the road, and they hadn't expected they would need water.

"Hang in, Joey . . . patience," he got closer to his moaning brother and realized he'd just said something wrong. His brother hated that all-too-familiar word, and now Valius only wanted to say something his brother liked.

"Drink," repeated the shepherd boy, and he licked his lips that were covered in dry blood.

Valius stomped his feet, squeezing the edge of the wagon and looking at Alex in confusion. Alex gritted his teeth and silently forged ahead, without turning back to look at the moaning child.

"Drink," pleaded the little boy in a weak voice.

"Take over the reins!" said Alex suddenly, and he started running to a farm up the nearby hill.

Valius ran around the wagon, grabbed the loose reins, and pulled them the same way Alex had a moment before. Having something to do made it easier for him to hear his brother's moaning. His mind was busy too because he had to closely watch the road to avoid the wheels hitting a stone or sinking into a hole. Valius preferred moaning to silence; at least he could hear that his brother was alive. Also, it seemed that the bleeding had stopped. Mrs. Nakutis had crossed herself just a little too early.

"Little Joe cannot die, he must not die," thought Valius. "If only we can get him to Kraziai alive . . ."

The wagon had almost made it to the top of the hill when Alex returned with a cup of water. But little Joe was no longer thirsty; he was drifting off. Carefully, Valius stuck a finger between his brother's teeth, bringing the cool cup to the boy's lips. A narrow stream of water ran down the shepherd's cheek.

"Drink, Joey, drink," begged Valius, as if his brother's entire life hung on this drop of water. If only little Joe would drink, he would survive.

Joe drank. The child's small Adam's apple visibly moved. Joe took a deep breath and licked his lips.

V

“Where should I turn?” asked Valius, hearing the first cobblestones of Kraziai under the wagon wheels. The cobblestones knocked the wagon around, and Joe started moving and moaning in pain. They both looked worried. They’d never driven a patient. Kraziai had no hospital, and they didn’t know where patients were taken in Kraziai.

“To the pharmacy,” decided Alex. He had been to the pharmacy before. The pharmacist would know what to do with wounded people.

The aged pharmacist shook his head. “Where are you bringing him?”

Alex lifted Joe again, the boy’s head resting on Alex’s shoulder.

“What are you doing, people?” scolded the pharmacist hopelessly. “How can I help him —?”

“So where, then?” demanded Alex, answering in a deep voice and looking sternly at the pharmacist. He’d already laid the little boy on the floor and stood up.

“He needs a doctor,” begged the pharmacist. “A doctor,” he added after a brief pause, “if he is still able to help . . .”

The pharmacist’s wife came out to the sounds of the commotion. An elderly woman, she had gray hair, sunken cheeks, and large, sadly kind eyes. She instinctively shut her eyes at her first look at the floor and leaned against the wall. "Maybe we should call Casper?" she offered quietly.

"How would a nurse help him? We need Dr. Schmidt, don't you see?" said the pharmacist.

The pharmacist's wife did see. She saw both the need for Dr. Schmidt and her husband's agitation. Nobody was allowed to call for Dr. Schmidt . . . unless he happened to come on his own. Nobody could have anything to do with him. The woman leaned against the wall, rubbing her temples with her thin hands and trying to focus. She looked at the floor again. She seemed afraid.

"Maybe I can run quickly across the gardens," she thought aloud.

The pharmacist said nothing in reply. The new rules were strict and made no sense. You could not sell medications to a Jew, and you could not treat a Jew, but you could probably call a Jewish doctor for help. After all, they'd left Dr. Schmidt alive for a reason; otherwise, he would be already dead in the Kupres woods along with all the others. Maybe calling Dr. Schmidt to help was not such a big offense, although running for Casper would be a safer choice. Let Casper call for the Jew if Casper was unable to treat people.

Suddenly the bell above the pharmacy's door jingled. A tall, broad-shouldered, somewhat stout man energetically entered the pharmacy. He looked young, less than thirty-five years old.

"What's going on?" The newly arrived man uttered his usual greeting, as if he really didn't know. Without looking at anyone, he hurriedly donned the medical smock handed to him by the pharmacist while listening to Valius's recount.

"When did it happen?" Dr. Schmidt interrupted Valius calmly. "How did you bring him here?"

The doctor's voice was clear and his language was pure. There was nothing Jewish about him. His hair curled right next to the skin, but then it was totally straight and carefully combed upward. He seemed concerned, as he usually was when visiting a patient, and he was also intensely upbeat, which helped him mask his own anxiety.

"Go get Casper," the doctor said, not addressing anyone in particular, while he still carefully examined his patient. "One person would not be able to manage here."

This time the pharmacist himself hurried off to get the assistant. For Casper, there was no need to sneak around the gardens. Then again, the pharmacist would avoid staying around the Jew. His wife could find all the medications just as well. Politics had always been safer for women. The authorities never suspected women as much as they suspected men.

Dr. Schmidt asked for a syringe, delivered an injection, and began washing the wounds carefully.

"It looks bad," he observed, lifting his gaze for the first time and looking Alex straight in the eye. "His eyes are gone . . . and on the right hand, only one little finger is left."

Knitting his brows, he looked at little Joe's hand for a long while. He looked at Alex again. "Yes, yes . . . the little finger can still be saved. No need to amputate it. Tell them this at the hospital . . . Make sure you tell them!"

Alex looked at the doctor's eyes, hearing none of his words. The eyes looked strange, like eyes he'd never seen before. They were large and dark and deep, like bottomless black pools. Alex felt uncertainty in that pool, a childish need for approval.

Alex hastened to nod his head in agreement. "Yes, yes, no need to cut off the little finger." His mind registered the word "hospital." Why would they need a hospital? Couldn't Dr. Schmidt manage by himself?

"Will he live?" Valius fearfully asked, his voice trembling. The doctor only shook his head energetically, without looking at Valius. The patient had to be taken to Raseiniai right away. He needed to be admitted to an emergency room. His wounds were very serious, but his life was not in danger. Unless, of course, the wounds got infected.

The doctor tended Joe while squatting next to him. "How did you bring him? In a wagon?" he asked and shook his head. "You can't drive the boy to Raseiniai in a wagon. It will knock and shake him around, and he may lose too much blood. He needs a car to get to Raseiniai —only by car. Is there any kind of transport going to Raseiniai right now?"

The pharmacist's wife joined in. "There are no passenger cars traveling to Raseiniai. Vaclovas Stulginskis drives people in his truck. Maybe we can ask him."

Alex and Valius hurried out to look for Stulginskis. It was better to be somewhere else doing something rather than standing in the pharmacy looking at the wounded child and the feverishly working doctor.

A war was the biggest magician of all. It turned cities into piles of ruins in a second. It turned streets into graveyards and bare fields, wealthy people into beggars, and the healthy . . . into helpless cripples. The also war made some people happy in a second, turning a beggar into a rich man, an insignificant little man who was used to be pushed around and chronically disdained into a city master.

Vaclovas Stulginskis had found his fortune, an unreachable dream, on the second day of the war in a ditch, upside down. It was a used truck, a one-and-a-half-ton Russian truck. Stulginskis was a driver and a skillful mechanic. A truck was just the thing that had been missing in his life. Oblivious to the German soldiers driving by and the scattered shots, he'd hired a couple of horses and dragged the truck into his father's barn that same June evening.

A few days later, he'd visited his cousin and shared his plan with him. The cousin, whom the war had transformed into a mighty policeman who proudly wore a white band on his arm, would help Stulginskis register the car in the name of Kraziai police, so that the Germans would not complain about a missing trophy truck. In exchange, Stulginskis would drive the truck whenever the police asked him.

Summoned by a policeman in the middle of the night, Vaclovas Stulginskis would start the engine and quickly drive to police headquarters. He'd pay no attention to his cargo; it could be people, their belongings, or cattle. He didn't care where he drove; an armed policeman always sat next to him giving directions. Stulginskis would treat the policeman to a cigarette, chat with him, and ask him to leave some of the transported belongings in the truck for himself. He made sure he appeared humble to his nosy neighbors. "It's not my business . . . you do not argue with the police. They expect their orders to be carried out. It's wartime."

He'd never told anyone about his nightly rides transporting Jewish men and women to the Kupres woods. He hadn't known any details, as his orders were to drive ahead and then stop near the Karalienes highway. As to where those Jews were taken from there—to work or somewhere else—that wasn't his business. Nikodemas Nakutis would just wave his hand at him, rushing him out of there to spare him seeing those details.

The Kraziai police force was small and didn't need much driving. The low-ranking policemen could walk on foot, leaving Stulginskis plenty of time to make his own trips to Raseiniai, Taurage, Kaunas, and Siauliai. There were no passenger cars available, but people had lots of business to attend to, mostly in the unusually busy black market. No car suited such tasks better than a police car. The war had truly made Vaclovas Stulginskis happy and rich.

Sweating, Alex and Valius returned from Stulginskis's home empty-handed. The driver and his truck had gone to Kaunas and were not expected back until the evening. The only vehicle in town should not be expected to stand idle during such times.

The street was empty, its pavement clean and seldom used. A small sand cloud formed above the ground in a breeze. Couch grass peeked out between the cobblestones. The little town was empty too. Most of its inhabitants were already resting in the Kupres woods.

Alex and Valius walked aimlessly on the street pavement, lost in their thoughts and not knowing what to do next. The doctor wanted them to rush to Raseiniai but forbade using the wagon, and Mrs. Nakutis was waiting for them at the farm. Such a day! The rye was as dry as gunpowder. Every hour counted. In his mind, Alex could see his mistress running to the gate and looking for him in anger.

"Valius, you stay here," said Alex, "while I head back. I can't help here anyway, and the old lady will get furious."

Valius would have liked Alex to stay with him. What would Valius do? How would he talk alone with Stulginskis? He needed money to hire a vehicle, but he didn't have the nerve to ask Alex for anything else. Mrs. Nakutis had already been too nice to let them use her horses on such a day. Mr. Nakutis would never agree to it. "The dogs must go to the dogs," Mr. Nakutis would laugh with his mocking, scowling, and piercing eyes.

"Let's go in and take a last look," suggested Valius timidly to his older friend, fearing

Alex's departure would leave him behind like a thin hop plant that the wind had torn away from its base.

Dr. Schmidt and Casper were still attending to little Joe. The pharmacist stood behind the counter while his wife leaned against the doorpost. Alex and Valius stopped at the entryway, looking at the hands of the doctor and his assistant, busy stretching ribbons of sparkling white bandage. Joe had no eyes, no forehead, no cheeks, no neck, no hands. Just a large white bundle lay on the floor—and long, thin legs stuck out from the bundle, scratched by stubbles, chapped, and covered by dry mud that had accumulated over several days. Only two openings were left in the place that used to be Joe's face, one for the nose and another for the mouth.

Dr. Schmidt listened to Joe's breathing from time to time, leaning down to the boy's chest. All eyes focused on the doctor listening to Joe's breathing, but the man's face was hard to read.

"No truck?" he asked, looking into Alex's eyes. He avoided other eyes, and other eyes avoided him too.

"He will return only in the evening," replied Alex hoarsely.

The doctor rolled up the sleeve of his smock. He lifted his arm to check the hour, looking at a shining gold wristwatch. Visibly concerned, he remained speechless. Nobody asked the doctor for the time. The sun had hardly crossed its zenith. It was lunchtime, yet nobody was thinking about lunch at this moment. Six people stood speechless in the room, each to their own thoughts. No force could possibly bring them together and make them talk to one another.

An unconscious shepherd lay on the pharmacy floor. He was fighting for his life, and nobody could help him. Yet lips were tight, not because of the shepherd and not because of his life-threatening condition.

There was something far more horrible, more powerful and mysterious, as it had no name. The shadow of death that hovered over the injured child was not as scary and not as terrible in comparison to the dreadful and unseen ghost now floating slowly among the healthy. Nobody talked about it. Yet the silence was as frightening as talking about it.

"I don't want to go up the hill!" the shepherd interrupted the strained silence in a high alto. "I don't want to! It's dark up there."

Thrashing around, little Joe tried to move his bandaged arms and lift his head.

The doctor jumped to Joe's side, holding his head and quietly ordering, "Get some water."

The doctor's face did not look as concerned as before, showing signs of incipient, comforting hope.

The door swung wide-open, bumping Valius across his back, and a woman appeared at the doorstep. She seemed out of breath and desperate, her headscarf sliding off onto her shoulders and her thin, bedraggled braid nearly coming undone.

"Joseph! My child!" cried the woman, stretching her arms toward her son from a distance and trying to ignore the wave of terror approaching her. But the terror had already arrived. It made her stumble and clouded her eyes with thick fog. The woman's knees gave out, and she slid into an invisible hole, suddenly losing her balance.

Valius and Alex managed to catch her, but it was hard to hold her up.

"Syringe!" jumped the doctor. He grabbed her hand, looking for her pulse. The old woman's entire body broke out in small quivers, her head hanging down helplessly on her chest.

"Lay her down right next to Joe. You won't manage to hold her up much longer," instructed Casper. Only her right hand seemed to obey her mind; her tightly clenched fingers were digging into a white, knotted handkerchief, with the small knot apparently containing her entire year's savings.

“Take her home. Her heart will not hold here,” said Dr. Schmidt while preparing a hurried injection.

The mother calmed down after the injection. Her breath resembled that of child who had been crying for too long, inhaling quickly and slowly exhaling, while interrupting herself often. Her right hand relaxed and released the handkerchief with the knot, dropping it onto the floor. Alex picked it up by the knot and, without looking at it, handed it to Valius.

“You wait for the truck,” Alex said, barely moving his lips to prevent the woman on the floor from hearing him. “I will bring her home while she is still unconscious.” Then he added after a short pause, “And you also pay the doctor if there is any money left in there.”

“Is there enough?” Valius was worried.

“Quiet, you people,” remarked the doctor curtly. “There will be enough time for payment. Take the mother.” He looked at his watch again and loudly announced the time. “It’s four o’clock.”

“Dinnertime,” the pharmacist noted weakly from behind the counter, barely masking his wish to have everybody leave the pharmacy or at least get away himself.

“Careful, let me help you.” The doctor’s assistant jumped to Alex and Valius as they lifted the woman from the floor. He too was happy for a chance to leave the pharmacy.

"The child must not be moved," decided the doctor, speaking to nobody in particular. "I will stay with him," he added, sitting in an unstable chair near the window.

"Then perhaps I should not lock the pharmacy?" hesitated the pharmacist, glancing at his wife and at Dr. Schmidt. After all, he and Dr. Schmidt had known each other for a very long time. Was he likely to steal anything from the pharmacy? They'd never had any conflicts in the past . . .

VI

The sixteen-year-old boy slept on a narrow bench that had been brought to him the evening before by the pharmacist's wife. He was curled up uncomfortably, his knees almost touching his chin. Perhaps he was used to sleeping wherever he found a spot. Having fought against evil known only to him just half an hour earlier, the shepherd had at last calmed down and rested. The doctor seemed convinced that the boy would survive at least until the morning.

They had been unable to get the truck the previous evening. Vaclovas Stulginskis had refused to drive anywhere at night. The war laws were strict—the Germans might stop him, he might lose the truck, and he might get into trouble himself. They would be fine driving in the morning. The truck would go to Kaunas the next morning anyway.

The pharmacist had left without wishing them good night. He'd pointed to a candle stub, left a few matches, and walked out, his eyes looking down. He'd locked the door to his room. He hadn't remembered ever locking it before. He actually used to leave it ajar to hear the pharmacy downstairs.

Dr. Schmidt sat in an unstable chair, his shoulders leaning against the windowsill, his long legs stretched out. He almost enjoyed it here amid the familiar odor of medications, thinking that any minute he might be needed for his wounded patient. He would not be able to sleep like that at home. He had not slept for many nights. At home, he paced in his room and smoked. His wife, hearing his steps from another room, did not sleep either. Occasionally opening the door, he could see her watching Ben, their seven-year-old son, quietly breathing in his sleep. She might catch some sleep tonight, as she wouldn't be hearing him pacing.

She shouldn't worry. She always completely trusted her husband. He had sworn to her, many times, that nothing bad could happen to them. After all, had anything happened to them so far? They had not been herded to the Kupres woods along with the others, had they?

Reverend Bumbulis, the pastor of Kraziai, had assured them personally that they could not leave such a large population without a doctor, especially at such times. Bumbulis had convinced the chief of the Kraziai police to wait a bit, just until the occupation authorities had made their decision. The pastor had even written a letter to the archbishop, pleading for his Excellency to intervene. Kraziai must have a doctor. Dr. Schmidt was so dedicated to his work and loved by all people. Besides, he had practically become Lithuanian, and he was even prepared to convert to Catholicism. The pastor had clearly emphasized the words "practically become Lithuanian" by underscoring them.

"We must win some time," the pastor had comforted them. "You must survive somehow, just until the first madness blows away."

In the pastor's opinion, they should use everything they had to save their lives. Gold, expensive things. The chief of police was notorious for his greed—and so was his father-in-law, only greedier. Bribery would gain time, until the archbishop would provide mercy. Then everything would pass. It was just some kind of temporary misunderstanding; people must have gone crazy because of their sins.

Dr. Schmidt had nodded his head in agreement with Reverend Bumbulis, swearing to his wife that the reverend must have been telling sacred truth. Yet Dr. Schmidt had gained no solace for his belief. As night descended, something had come to talk with the doctor. It had no name. It could have been a thought, a premonition, a fear of inevitability. He had never been superstitious and had never thought much about mysticism. The secret worlds of spirits had seemed to him the ridiculous fruit of the imaginations of people with weak nervous systems. Even Dostoyevsky seemed to him distant and unnatural. Had his nerves gone weak? Had he become incurably ill too? Without a doctor in Kraziai, who would treat him? Besides, how would he leave Kraziai? He would be shot at the first crossroad.

Perhaps he wasn't alone in his madness. Could it be that all those people he knew so well had all gone mad? Some sort of infection must have set in along with the German tanks. He no longer recognized the people he knew, and nobody recognized him.

Right now he remained the only Jewish male in Kraziai. Everyone he knew had turned away from him as he walked along the edge of the pavement of an empty street. He was not allowed to use the sidewalk. He was not allowed to slip by a fence quietly, unnoticed like a thief, avoiding meeting other people—other people who fear him. No, he must be visible to all. It was illogical reality.

Spotting him, the children scurried to hide behind fences and watch him, their eyes wide-open with terror, curiosity, and hatred. A big, broad-shouldered, healthy young man had overnight turned into a frightening ghost, a poltergeist with no right to be among the living. This incomprehensible change, an impossible metamorphosis, had driven him insane—in spite of his young, healthy, and strong nervous system.

An insane man banged his head against the wall or ran in the fields, holding it with both hands. An insane man running in the fields must leave behind everything he owned. He must forget he had anything at all, even if he had only a few worthless possessions. Only then can he run away. But Dr. Schmidt had much more than a few worthless possessions. He had a wonderful wife, his beautiful Esther, who'd left her rich parents in Kaunas and followed him to this poor town, even before officially marrying him. He also had Ben, his son, who was only seven years old but already could read and write Lithuanian.

His blue-eyed son didn't even know he was Jewish. He didn't suspect that the land where he was born, along with many children just like him, had no right to raise him. No, before the change, his son had known nothing about this. But now everything—every cobblestone—screamed to him about his trouble. Ben was too young to understand it all, and he just cried like all children do. When Dr. Schmidt finally went insane and started running across the fields, even Reverend Bumbulis would no longer try to convince him that this land and these Christians had any use at all for his wife and his child.

Eighty children were now locked up in the barn of the Siuksta manor behind the bridge. Their parents had been taken to the Kupres woods last week, and only five Jewish women were left alive to take care of them. The barn had gotten contaminated with dysentery. He had gone there, but the guards had not allowed him near the children. He'd pleaded and begged the guards, telling them that he was a doctor and that his place was with the sick. A thin-faced man with a wild gypsy look and a white armband stared at him and snickered, "You are a Yid. Your place is in the Kupres woods."

During sleepless nights, he'd kept thinking about his right place. A strange voice had kept bringing up "Kupres woods." Yes, the pastor had been right; he had practically become Lithuanian. He'd rarely spoken Yiddish. He hadn't congregated with the town's businessmen or tradesmen. He'd read Lithuanian newspapers and books, and he'd sent his son to a Lithuanian kindergarten. He'd taken pride in his wife's Aryan looks, her blue eyes and light hair.

Now it all seemed a child's self-deceptive mistakes. The stubborn Jewish national fatalism used to irritate him. He used to hate the self-restraint, the deep distrust of other people, and the melancholy apparent in the weary eyes of the bearded patriarchs. During these one and a half months since the Germans had arrived, he too had turned into an old man, burdened by this gigantic three-thousand-year-old weariness of his nation.

Perhaps he could hide somewhere along with his wife and his son? Just for a couple of weeks or months? Sometimes, in the hot August sun, he had been beset by an unusual yearning to go into hiding, to seek safety, to live just anywhere else at any cost, to look for any kind of support, to connect with people fighting against this nightmare and brutality. After all, such people must exist somewhere. Yet he'd felt an unbearable and irrevocable conviction, which lay on and pressed him down with its inhuman weight as soon as he stepped onto the pavement to cross a street, all alone, not spoken to by anyone, escorted by frightened looks. At home, he'd used all his willpower to look upbeat and keep his wife from sensing the true extent of his desperation.

During the day, he'd walked around as a finely tuned musical instrument carefully prepared for an important concerto; he'd applied exaggerated energy and diligence with every patient that still trusted him or was forced to trust him. Everybody had trusted him only a month and half ago. Everybody from young to old had trusted him.

Yet now he read suspicion and superstitious fear in the eyes of almost every patient. Might the condemned Jew lie and poison them out of hatred and revenge? Rumor had it that the Jews poisoned wells at night and contaminated small towns with infectious diseases. Could, for instance, Dr. Schmidt destroy them slowly and surreptitiously by making an injection laced with pernicious bacteria or poison?

Some dark forces were so terribly strong that, once awakened, they created waves that were nearly impossible to resist. If only all people would rise together and say no to violence, then everything would stop—the live and burning hearts would restrain and subdue the bloody force all at once. Yet for some reason, the hearts fearfully crouched down and shrank, and people got swept into that wave. A paralysis of conscience, an attack of fear took hold of people and they were unable to resist any longer—and they fell, downed by the wave, or helplessly allowed themselves to be swept away by it.

This wave of dark violence must have had something devilishly tempting, poisonously attractive, that lured many people and befuddled their minds. What was it? An atavism of the human animal, the revenge of animal instincts against the centuries-long self-liberation of humanity from their terrible rule? Was it avarice? Was it an orgy of passions that yearned for the most bestial satisfaction and self-defilement?

While in medical school in Kaunas, Dr. Schmidt had tried to understand the nature of German fascism and spent long hours discussing and arguing with Jewish doctors who had escaped from Königsberg, driven by the events of 1933. Apparently he had been too young then to understand all of this. Perhaps, even at his age now, he wouldn't be able to understand it all just by reading books, talking to others, or even listening to his own abstract deliberations.

This nightmare could only be understood through personal experience—that is, unfortunately, a belated understanding. This understanding helped nothing when you were walking all alone on rough-stoned pavement, wearing a humiliating and condemning yellow star, when everybody around feared and superstitiously avoided you, and you started fearing yourself too for some strange reason—and you almost believed that such must be the fate of your entire nation, which you must share, and you might not and must not divert or betray.

"Your place is in the Kupres woods," tossed a predatory killer in your face, and you were incapable of fighting or convincing even yourself that this was a terrible injustice and most shameless violence. You couldn't fight or argue, not only because you were afraid of dying but also because of a greater fear, a more mysterious fear of betraying those who were already lying there in the Kupres woods, under the huge pine trees. This was impossibly absurd and irrevocably real.

Didn't you hear somebody inviting you to visit the Kupres woods at night? Just for a quick look . . . Was that somebody standing right here, right now, between you and this wounded child who might not survive until morning? Was that somebody, at this very moment, closer to the child or to you?

The doctor jumped out from his chair, stretching up and shivering lightly through his entire body. It would be nice to take a couple of steps forward right now and feel his body alive, strong, and moving. But right next to him lay the agonizing and unconscious shepherd boy, the morning chill numbing the child's bare feet. And then, even closer to the doctor, cheek to cheek, Dr. Schmidt felt the presence of that immovable and unavoidable something, which he could not push or even shove away with his chest.

That something was not a wall, or a rock, or a tree; it was a being with its own will and purpose. If he could only shake it and yell at it angrily and loudly, "Why are you here? What on earth do you need?" But the doctor did not yell. He had not gone mad yet, and he was still able to control his nerves. He had to compose himself, diverting his thoughts away from that mercilessly senseless question, which had been torturing him for a month and a half already. The doctor knew it was a very short question: “When?” Yet he did not ask it aloud, fearing that something might hear him and reply clearly and mercilessly: “Now. Right away.”

He brought himself to squat near the wounded child, taking his hand to read his pulse out loud. The child’s mouth appeared black in the gray dusk of the incipient morning. Yet the black mouth was still breathing. It inhaled air greedily while the boy’s pulse was beating evenly, better than the previous evening. The little shepherd might make it. His entire organism was straining to live, quickly making up the blood he’d lost. If only the hospital surgeons would not rush to amputate the entire palm of his right hand. It was still possible to save the small finger. If Dr. Schmidt were only allowed to come along with the wounded boy to Raseiniai, he would help save it. It was so important to save the little finger! Only one little finger would prevent the boy from being handless. You couldn’t even begin to count the things one could do with just one little finger!

Dr. Schmidt let the child’s hand go and quickly stood up. He took a fountain pen out of his pocket, tore a page out of his notebook, and approached the pharmacy counter. He picked up the candlestick, tried to light it, then changed his mind and moved back near the window. Sitting down, he started writing on the sheet of paper that he'd placed on the windowsill. In the dim dawn light, he could barely see the letters: "Dear Colleague, Be as careful as possible. I am certain that the small finger . . ."

A soft but persistent knock at the pharmacy's door startled him. Dr. Schmidt stiffened in his chair and held his breath. The knock repeated, now louder and more insistent. "Must be using multiple knuckles," thought the doctor.

Valius swung his legs down from the bench and sat up, fearfully gazing at the doctor and still unable to recognize him. "Ah? Ah?" he uttered, unable to get himself together and preparing to making excuses for his tardiness.

"It's not for us," Dr. Schmidt whispered to him, leaning back to complete his writing in a shaking hand: " . . . can be saved."

He meant to sign it clearly, legibly, but this time too his signature came out in the usual professional doctor's style.

The door to the pharmacy shook because of heavy knocking—no more gentle knuckle knocking. The intruder knocked impatiently, using a heavy man's fists.

"Let us in, damn you! We'll take him anyway," echoed a deep, hoarse voice.

The pharmacist unlocked his bedroom door with a click. A candle dimly lit his face. It was sullen and confused. He hurried to the outside door, shuffling his slippers.

"Why hide . . . they seem to be looking for you . . . I told you to stay out for the night," the pharmacist mumbled to himself, looking down at his feet.

VII

A heavy August morning fog enveloped the entire small town. The houses and the trees loomed black and were hardly recognizable from ten steps away, looking like blurred, formless shadows. A bloody strip stood out in the darkness, far away on the barely identifiable horizon, preparing for the sun to rise soon. A rooster's crowing echoed hoarsely as the sound filtered through the thick fog.

Dr. Schmidt stood at the pharmacy doorstep and silently watched the two dark shadows in front of him. Black rifle barrels stuck out behind their backs. He saw nothing but these barrels, and he heard nothing but a deafening and threatening silence. The doctor did not know what he should say to these shadows. These days, he'd gotten used to not addressing anyone first. He'd gotten used to waiting.

But the black shadows too did not dare to disturb the silence. For some reason, these people seemed stunned by the ease of finding him, after having so furiously banged on the door in fear of him running away or hiding. The silence was so complete that the doctor thought he could hear the loud ticking of his watch. He lifted his wrist close to his eyes just to see the time. It was twenty-five minutes past five.

"Give it to me!" The biting order was spoken by the tall, skinny man with the gypsy face and black, piercing eyes that noticed everything around them. "Your time has come."

He grabbed the doctor's arm, squeezing his elbow with the thin, gripping fingers of his right hand, while deftly undoing the doctor's watchband with his left. The watch disappeared into his palm, without a trace, in a split second.

"Let's march, Mr. Schmidt," said a familiar deep voice, and the doctor noticed Nikodemas Nakutis's smirking, half-shut eyes.

Dr. Schmidt felt uneasy, as if he should say something to the familiar man or ask him something important, but the doctor was unable to open his mouth.

"There is a wounded child over here . . . he is nearly dying," the doctor whispered, excusing himself. "He needs to be sent to the hospital."

"Sure, somebody will send him," bellowed Mr. Nakutis's companion, getting hold of his rifle in a swift, sudden motion. "You go as you are told, and don't try anything smart."

Jurgis Meldutis looked disappointed or angered by something after sticking the watch into his pocket. The doctor made a hesitant step forward and stopped again, not knowing where to turn.

"To your home, the sweet home, Mr. Schmidt," explained Mr. Nakutis obligingly. "The sweet home . . . we will pick up your little wife, the kiddies, and then continue in no rush."

His deep voice appeared completely calm and friendly. He was not at all angry or afraid that the doctor might trick him. He even felt sympathy toward Dr. Schmidt, as the doctor would have to go to a place where nobody wanted to go.

The three men walked in the middle of street in the thick but quickly thinning fog. The sound of their big, manly steps echoed in the yards along the street. Dr. Schmidt walked in front. He hurried, trying to escape the hollow echo of the steps following him behind. That echo was frightening and haunting. Without the echo, he would feel no fear or anxiety.

"Don't run!" admonished Mr. Meldutis, speaking too loudly and slurring his words. He must have been drunk, judging from his slurring.

Running was not on the doctor's mind. Right now, almost nothing was on his mind. Or maybe there was a lot on his mind, but he was unable to understand his own thoughts. The thoughts appeared faster than his mind was able to form them. They appeared so fast, leaving such light traces in his memory, as if they were barely touching it with their fingertips. His home, his wife, his son, and the Kupres woods.

They would herd them on foot. It would be dusty. People would watch them from their backyards. It would be hard to bear their looks. The sun would be boiling hot. The pines would be tall and sparse. Sabakstynai. His wife would be afraid.

Why did he keep on swearing to her that Reverend Bumbulis would wait for the archbishop's letter? The children suffered from dysentery in the Siuksta barn. The little town was so empty. The steps too had never sounded so hollow. Why should he go home? Why did he keep on swearing to Esther? Did she believe him, or did she just pretend? Reverend Bumbulis also pretended that he was expecting the letter. What was the point of waiting for anything? Why did people always expect something? Expecting something was hope, and hope was pretense. Nice, noble, consoling. And others pretended to console him. He should have run away. The fear chased those who ran away. How badly would Esther be frightened? He should say something encouraging.

The doctor was unable to catch up with his thoughts and accelerated his step.

“Stop!” yelled Jurgis Meldutis. “You will miss your house.”

Dr. Schmidt had never thought that he was so big and his apartment door was so narrow. There was not even a doorstep to his bedroom. Why was Esther’s bed empty and rumpled? Why didn’t he first see her standing by the wall and hugging their son? Why were they both dressed up as if they had just now returned from a party?

Dr. Schmidt took a quick glance around the room and realized that somebody had messed up everything searching for something. The better things and clothes were piled on the floor between the beds. The chest doors were wide-open, and the drawers were pulled out.

“Esther!” he started apologizing, but his tongue remained stuck to the roof of his mouth, while his wife’s eyes begged him to tell her nothing, begged for no more explaining. Let Reverend Bumbulis continue expecting a letter from his bishop . . .

He had never noticed such indescribable tranquility and infinite devotion reflected in his wife’s face. Why was it that she had never before seemed so knowledgeable, all understanding, and ready for anything?

“Let’s go,” whispered Dr. Schmidt, reaching for his son’s hand.

The little boy was shivering. His eyes opened wide and filled with terror. But they had no tears. No, his son would not scream. Both his wife and his son were much smarter than he'd assumed.

"Let's go," repeated the doctor quietly, looking at his wife in fascination and appreciation.

"Take along your things!" ordered Nikodemas Nakutis, pointing at the pile of clothes between the beds. "Tie them up and take them with you."

"Perhaps you expect us to carry them for you?" yelled Jurgis Meldutis sarcastically.

They talked very strangely. They must have been mocking Dr. Schmidt and his family. Or maybe the pastor had finally received a letter from the archbishop? No, that was nonsense . . . what had the pastor to do with this?

Nikodemas Nakutis and Jurgis Meldutis helped them tie the clothes. The two men stuffed into the bundles everything they had pulled out of the chest. They worked fastidiously, more so than the owners who would have to carry these bundles somewhere.

"We will go," repeated Dr. Schmidt again, suddenly feeling a sense of relief. He was holding a heavy bundle in one hand and the boy's hand in the other.

"Where are we going?" asked Ben in a whisper.

"To the woods," explained his father, against his better intention.

Strangely, Dr. Schmidt did not fear his unexpected words. Instinctively, he squeezed the boy's fingers in his hand. It seemed that the child's hand too was trying to mold into his father's hand as deeply as possible. Nobody had ever trusted him so unconditionally.

"Walk next to us," the doctor told his wife, bending under the weight of the bundle. "Don't lag behind."

Mr. Nakutis was again beyond the doctor's understanding, directing them away from the Kupres woods. He pointed them to the river, to the bridge across the Krazante. Could it be possible that they were being taken to the children who were sick with dysentery in the large barn at the Siuksta manor, where the doctor was so badly needed?

A clear thought lit up in the doctor's mind —the first clear, even, bright, and deeply etched thought in his mind since he'd seen the shadows with rifle barrels this morning in the fog. Perhaps he could still save his son. At least his son!

His feet sank into the sand of a small side street. He had to slow down, had to let those two with the rifles come closer.

"Mr. Nakutis." For the first time, the doctor addressed the familiar man who had invited him for dinner at his home just half a year before. “Mr. Nakutis! I treated your daughter . . .” He couldn’t continue talking. He didn’t realize that the simplest words could fill his eyes with tears. “I did everything I could,” he forced himself to continue. “I did more than I could . . . save my son . . . let him join the other children . . . in the manor . . .”

The sand under his feet made a hollow, crunchy sound. It kept on crunching dully and monotonously. Yet Mr. Nakutis remained silent. His ever piercing and mocking eyes were fixed on the crunching sand that was disturbing the morning tranquility.

“Mr. Nakutis . . .” The doctor sensed the pity in his begging voice, unable to stay silent.

“Stop howling,” yelled the man with the gypsy face. “We are not allowed to talk with the Yids.”

Mr. Nakutis heard Mr. Meldutis yell and brought his eyes up from the ground. “There is no point discussing this matter, Mr. Schmidt,” he calmly explained. “The Germans said not a single Yid would remain in the world. The Germans do not engage in idle talk.”

The wooden bridge across the Krazante River creaked under their feet with a hollow sound, as if in agreement with Mr. Nakutis’s deep voice and his calm, unalterable decision. The doctor squeezed his son’s hand even harder. The squeeze indicated that he had done everything he possibly could to help forestall the terrifying thought, which would soon reach his son's mind. The entire palm of his hand felt his son's live, strong, and healthy pulse throbbing in his every little finger.

They had almost reached Medziokalnis. The tall pine trees and the linden trees with widely spread branches appeared slowly as the fog cleared away. Medziokalnis had always been the amusement site for the small town. The young people used to dance in its flat clearing on Sundays to the accompaniment of an accordion.

"I don't want to go up the hill!" the wounded shepherd had shouted yesterday, hallucinating in fever. What would his scream have to do with Medziokalnis? The doctor did not try to fathom the meaning. The shepherd had not been screaming words; this was just an endless, persistent, and depressing ear pressure. "I don't want to go up the hill!"

But nobody forced them to go up the hill. Jurgis Meldutis, unstable on his feet, pointed to the gravel pits dug at the foot of the hill. Their shoes sank into the gravel, small stones rolling from under their feet. A large square hole had been dug down in the gravel pit. It was so large, it would be too comfortable for the three members of the Schmidt family.

“Place your things over here,” commanded Meldutis, showing no discomfort. “Put them down . . . and go next to the hole.”

He watched for some time the three people who were stuck in the freshly dug gravel. Then, losing his patience and unable to restrain himself any longer, he ran up to Dr. Schmidt, greedily grabbed the flap of his jacket, and began carefully fingering its fabric.

“Undress!” commanded Mr. Nakutis.

Dr. Schmidt had heard about undressing Jews before shooting them down. He was not at all surprised. A sudden, intense, and nearly uncontrollable rage came over him. He thought of Esther, of her smooth white skin, flexible, curved waist, and slim legs—never before, he could swear, exposed to another man.

“Hide behind me,” he told his wife, spreading out his arms and slipping off his jacket, as if he could, with this single motion, cover the nakedness of his beloved woman forever.

“Should I take off my clothes too?” asked the little boy pitifully, without comprehending.

Nobody answered him. His father painfully bit his lip until it bled. It would be better if he screamed . . . his son . . .

Running, Izidorius Martinkus reached Kraziai just in time, before the truck's departure. His mother had sent him out. She'd had a feeling that Valius alone would not be able to convince Stulginskis to drive, and, upon reaching Raseiniai, he wouldn't know where to go with such a seriously wounded patient.

The sun was already high up. It was wading through the fog—large, white, bathed in dew, awakening the small town. It was not alone in waking up the town. The first shots were heard from Medziokalnis at dawn, and now they continued in long barrages. Awakened, townspeople opened their windows carefully and listened fearfully.

Valius and Izidorius Martinkus listened too, standing at the pharmacy doorstep. When the shots died off, they heard the truck engine unable to start, sneezing and buzzing with no rhythm, from over ten houses away.

"Will it start?" Izidorius stamped his feet impatiently.

Valius did not feel like talking and thinking. He was cowering because of the cool fog and an uncontrollable shiver over his entire body. He only wanted to leave as soon as possible, disappear from Kraziai, escape from that fear and anxiety that Dr. Schmidt had left behind upon walking out with

Nikodemas Nakutis and Jurgis Meldutis. He was afraid that Mr. Nakutis and Mr. Meldutis might return to find out who had sat with Dr. Schmidt in the pharmacy all night long. The doctor's note in Valius's pocket was too important to throw away and too dangerous to keep.

"Finally," rejoiced Izidorius. "If only he would take us along." The truck appeared on the street and rolled along the pavement. "If only he would take us," repeated Izidorius in his mind, stepping out to the middle of the street. Should he miss the truck, he wouldn't know what to do with his wounded brother, where to call for assistance. Who would give a horse for two days?

But Vaclovas Stulginskis stopped the truck. He was angry, nervous, and very unhappy. "So hurry up and bring him on quickly!" he hollered without getting out of the truck.

A pile of sacks lay in the truck bed close to the cabin, and three women sat on them. They spread out over their sacks so that nobody could touch them.

Izidorius considered asking them to move the sacks over to the end of the truck bed to make room for his brother closer to the cabin. Judging from their hostile looks, the women were determined to protect their sacks, so he didn't dare to ask for anything. He shifted his weight from foot to foot, barely holding onto his unconscious teenage brother.

“Lay him down already! What are you waiting for?” Mr. Stulginskis’ cousin jumped out of the cabin wearing a white armband.

Another loud barrage of shots was heard from the direction of Medziokalnis. Without turning off the engine, Mr. Stulginskis too jumped out of the cabin. He listened attentively, turning toward Medziokalnis.

“Ah, they are whacking the Yid’s kids,” said Mr. Stulginskis angrily. It was hard to judge if he was upset by the shooting or just by his inability to watch it closely.

“You saw, they took the doctor too,” whispered one woman to her neighbor. They exchanged frightened looks and then turned to the bandaged shepherd and his bare, bluish feet as he was being placed into the truck.

“Go already!” yelled the cousin to the truck owner. “What can you hear anyway?”

“Hold his head,” instructed one of the women. “Lift it onto your lap, otherwise it will get banged around.”

“I hope they don’t stop us at Kryzkalnis,” fearfully whispered another woman, turning her head and squinting her eyes over her shoulder to the road ahead.

“Hold his head tightly,” repeated the first woman angrily, pulling her feet under her so that the wounded boy would not accidentally roll over them.

"Lord help us," sighed the woman looking at the road. She lowered her eyes and quickly, almost furtively, crossed herself.

"The truck's moving," said Valius with childish relief.